Collected Verse of
Cecile Norma Musson
Volumes I, II, and III

Collected Verse of
Cecile Norma Musson

Volumes I, II, and III

Cecile Norma Musson

Ivy House
Publishing Group
www.ivyhousebooks.com

PUBLISHED BY IVY HOUSE PUBLISHING GROUP
5122 Bur Oak Circle, Raleigh, NC 27612
United States of America
919-782-0281
www.ivyhousebooks.com

ISBN: 1-57197-442-3
Library of Congress Control Number: 2004116313

Printed in the United States of America

For
Dear Cousin Fannie
Who on the knee at age two placed me
to learn my ABC
Starting me on my journey of love with WORDS.

I wish to express my deepest thanks to the International Biographical Centre of Cambridge, England with whom my long relationship was instrumental in my receiving your good selves as my publisher at their suggestion.

Volume I

Song of a Woman

Song of a Woman

I Sing
The Song of a Woman
And I Am
All the Daughters of Mother Eve

Joy is a mountain
Sleep is a sea
Climbing high I dive deep
Deep into the effortless waters of Sleep
Or, are they grayly opaque those
Waters of Sleep?
Gray and warm and kissful of my Being.
Sweet, deep waters! Would I were conscious of them
while I swim them. But, no, only waking I know them.
Only waking can I joy in having slept.
Why not conscious of Sleep's joy?
Why not till dawn's silver sword or golden
Cuts the web that binds my eyelids to unconsciousness?
Of Death, I want consciousness of Death.
If not that, how then shall I know the long Sleep
Save by another awakening?
I plunge my hand into the stuff of Life—
Sleazy, bubbling, soiling stuff, reminding me
of a man's lifeblood I once saw in a congealed heap
before a hospital door—
fascinating, it repels: desirable, it sickens;
undeniable it is even though
it denies.
Lusty lures of the flesh gleam in the stuff.
I delay washing my spirit's thought clean for
the tempting moment when I think to smear
my Me with all of it at once.

To touch and leave for later taste
does not appeal.
No! Smear it now upon thy body—"And if it clog the spirit's
pores, smother
It's breath?"

Bah!
Let all go!
Abandon! Shriek with glee nude of bands no stops
no stays and in Youth's Age of Urgency
Eat all Up.

Two voices cry:
(1st Voice of Youth): "Think not to save for
staid old age, crippled-jointed
thy dance to make. For if the
urge remain may not the power.

(2nd Voice of Age): "Come back before you too far
stray across the line convention-set."
Bah!
Yet, in their day they flowers plucked across the way—
And suffered more than they enjoyed?

Three cups I must partake for balanced draught
Of life—
From cup of gold the spirit sup:
From silver for the mind;
While red in red I lusty gulp the body's portion—
each of itself a beauty to the sight and taste.
One draught of each a-mingling leaps through
singing veins
till to contain seems foolishness.
All must seek outlet.
Whisper counsels, "Wait! A MEETING in a fusion soon
will answer all thy lacks, rebellious, fears,
will supply true reason, sum and purpose

to thy years . . .
I dare not disbelieve!

Joy has made my body light so that I feel to soar,
scoop up a cloud on my way.
I love my love, love him more than mine own life.
Silver gleams brighter through the sheen of my mood;
flower colours leap with my aliveness.
Red soup in a green plate . . . I want to press the
colour to my breast, eat of its redness.
Oh, my mate! Take of my intellect, nourish me,
love me with yours.

In the midst of love
If I must write—then will my lover
hate my Pen.
I stay the indulgence of tears for words that tell
of them.
My food is interspersed with thoughts clamouring
paper.
I thought I loved once but no, I have loved
twice.
At the age of four, I fell in love with
WORDS—
I would be harlot for my Art's sake merely, and
virgin, and woman loved, and woman loving, unlov'd
and loved, unloving.
Then, I KNOW Eve's daughters. AM Eve's daughters.

Spring

Life is at the Spring
Life is in the tender green and none will be in tender green
Except I be in the green of them.
You will not live save
By now thundering heart
Future young girl:
The cord of birth is unbroken from Eve to me to you
All that is mine I hand inviolate to you
To me passed on from various—
The serpent's sting and Love's sting, the sting
Of many hungers.
The sweet of Spring! What sweeter than the
Sweet of Spring stinging my fertile, unimpregnated
Womb to foolishness. Caramba!
I live gloriously abandoned flood-water foolish
and powerful and the water and the blood of me
And I and my pen are one.
No lover can tear us apart—his body is not
Sufficient
No matter his masculine strength.
To tear a grafted tree is to kill
So I and my Pen,
Ink is in my veins
That makes me blue-blood. Ha!
I laugh like a child.

Ha! Ha! Ha!

When I laugh
I have the world
On my pinkie
a-twirl.

Never

When I was just age 16
Ahead of me, bent low, doddering along
An old woman, grey-haired
I,
passing by
Gave a short, sharp, derisive hoot
Of laughter
Singing a mocking song
For I knew
I,
being young
Could never be like that
For
I
Being young, am invincible.

War-Torn Fortys

I sit within the garden bower where bird and flower mingle blithe-ed-ly, Leaving, I leave the sacred place where Melody and Beauty handmaidens are to Peace out into the material war-torn world I turn. Yet, I take with me as bulwarks to my courage the knowledge of The Citadel where Christ is Prince of Peace and keeper of the key.

Canada

1945
Autumn's hand
has touched the land
leaves green now gold
or crimson
and some have leaves
like flowers of flame.

Glory Be

I have grasped the glory of Life
green and red and pulsating
under my hand.
In the midst of sorrow
I find reason to be exultant.
My inheritance is a golden, undying
Unkillable arrogance of heart
in the face of smashing Fate.
I battle the No of things, and
Swing them to my uses

And I and the God in me and Fate
And the tangle of things are one
And, despite it all
My soul and song enraptured be.

Play

In the hand of your Mind
Roll the Word around
Move it, push it, put it down
Take it up again
Because it teases you
You keep dropping it, it is too big,
Or too small.
Happily, you retrieve it
Because it has a beat
Happy with your feet.

My Mother

My mother, I and she
In perfect synchronicity
With my first life-flutter
In my womb-time
Swimming free
In amniotic fluid
That was when I came to be.

Refuge

I speak of Peace . . .
Come and rest awhile . . .
I sit in the deep, sweet stillness
Of the vast cathedral
while
the sun
at setting
sends its last yellow rays
through
the high windows.
As the flickering light
Caresses
The grey arches,
The organ sounds out like violins
Then dies into silence
with the dying light of day.
Blue-covered prayer books in the empty pews
with their red-edged leaves
Lend their liveliness to the scene.
As the outer light diminishes
The colours in the stained glass windows
Glow more brightly and
The Christ on the cross suffers more poignantly
While 'neath Him
Mary weeps more sadly
John's heart-compassion
For the Holy Mother grows.
The disciples watch from afar
And their self-abasement
For their own frailty
Grows keener.
Above all, God, the Father
Dies

With His begotten,
With Mary in her woe
And
Peter in self-condemnation.
As the organ rises to a pealing crescendo
The blues grow more vivid
And the reds almost bleed

While yellows and greens form sharper contrast.
Across the heart's silence the organ rolls,
now thunderous
Now exquisitely soft
So soft
That I grow breathless
Fearing to miss
Even the echo of a note.
Sharp
Across my exaltation
Comes the fear that the rhapsody
will end.

Agreed

The only way
I will survive this day
Is to repeated say:
"I'm fine. Fine. Fine."
I'll lie to myself and my self has no recourse
But to agree.

Ah! Hah!

With a zest and a zing
and a lilting swing
Here's to life.
With a twirl
And a twang
My soul it sang—
"Here's to Life!"

I am the swirl of the
Ocean wave
The up, the down
The round of it.

I am the spume that
Heavenward flies
I am the air
Surrounding it.

I in its disintegration
Am, the fall of it
And, in its renewal
Am, the all of it.

Memory

Memory sometimes is more sweet
Than that which remember
And summer's glorious sun more bright
When season brings December.

Que Sera Sera

I am ensnared
In the spider's web
Of steel-strong time.
Que sera sera. But what?
And I must wait
Without being told
"Turn here. Not there."
"Change about."
Where? Why?
Why not the I of me
To decide to be or not to be?

Of Queens and Kings

She walks queen proud
It matters not she scrubs
My floor for daily bread
Dainty, yet tall, the pail beside
Scrub brush in hand, no bride
More sweet, as by her feet
I joy to see her dignity . . .

There was another such
He my street sweeper was
No king vied with him.
My day he happier made
With smile and greeting
Always I looked t'ward our meeting,
The ruler of our land I held not
Higher in esteem.
He a king, she a queen.

All in All

My heart has eyes,
My heart has ears
With birds, I am their song
their flight, their joy
With trees,
I am their sway
their growth
their wideness
and their tallness.
And when they joy
At morning
With blossoms
I am in their dance
And even in their falling.

The Old Room . . .

The Old Room was very quiet and still
But swirling around in it were memories.
There had been four sisters. One had been ill in it. But before that, thousands of curls had been moaned over and exclaimed about. The high mirror glass had seen the skirts of dozens of evening dresses, the wearers on a chair to see it hung right.
All their tears had been wept in this room. Here, their inconsequential laughter, their gymnastics and one-act plays hilariously making imitations of others' idiosyncrasies, of broken English and each others' features and traits, Here, their conspiracies to get Mother to gentle Pa into Yes about a dance, a party or the silent movies.
Here, the dresses made at night in a flurry for 'Cup Match cricket, when they went more to be seen than to see. The diary jottings after about their conquests over the two-day heroes.
Here, the hidden heartbreak and the later laughter over a dead pain.
All their sonnets and stories had been sung and told here. A thousand stitches had darted through annoying silk stockings and organdy and lace and chiffon and warm tweed. The room had held brass and glass earrings and bracelets and necklaces and report cards and club mottoes and drawers that were the current draw-keeper's despair, tossed by a happy date-keeper.
There had been the smell of the sick (smelt for some time after) and there, was your own heartbreak then, when you were glad that sister's daughter asleep kept your tears from drowning you.

World War II Years . . .

A day can be a cruel thing—uncaring
The baby blue sky, the lavender and eggshell clouds
Are so aloof. The March wind never seems near
But is constantly heard in rattle of door and window
And seen in the wild bending of banana fronds
And twisted laundry on the line.
It does not care that a wild wind
Whips my mind to a froth.

The day stretches to the zenith, deepens to
The bottom of the sea and to the outermost of space.
What is my Beloved's day like?
Is he intrigued by accomplishment, or drearily
Accepting an unwelcome fate?
As with me does the treadmill go on of
Can't-Get-Away, Can't-Go-Forward
In this emotional situation?
This is a clock without hands. Timeless. Senseless
I am back to it again—this holding of my heart
In my Logic's hands to keep it from shattering
against the rock of Fate's miserliness.
Yet I am not ready for my Love—I must achieve
Some small success first.
I have since tried to hold my heart very still
So that neither Love nor Hate could sway it.

Avidly, greedily, I grab at Life. Hunger has quickened me.
Of the spiritual and mental parts I have exercised myself.
Now the sexual!
Now, all things be they spiritual or mental
Prod and prick the physical
Their expression, its expression, willy-nilly!

I must on to eat, to walk, to work, to play
And as I whip myself, my blood whips me, each the other—
this can only one way, Ha!
LOVE! . . . Love! . . . Love! And Always love
And, yet, never love . . .
Why should I forego the kiss of my lover
Kiss of the mouth or phallic kiss?
If my cry again should be
I *have not loved my lover*
I would feel drowned in foolishness
Yet does the mother-woman of me hold back
From the tears and insecurities of a love un-husbanded
For my text must ever be thus:
I. Peter 22.II, "Abstain from fleshly lusts that
war against the soul."
And also, St. Matthew 1:28, "And fear not them
which kill the body but are not able to kill the soul
But rather fear them which are able to destroy both soul and
body in hell."

Saving

Times I have rushed into the night
Whether moon or starlit, dark for me.
Times I have cried the blood from my very soul.
From my heart that beat but pain.
Only the strength of those who closely love me
Surging out in realizing love in those moments
Saved my beating brain and pain
Out upon the garden stones.
How their hearts would grieve at such a
Kind of death, alone save me

I have known the uttermost of sorrow—
Love, unloving, loving, unloved
Now I am come again to joy
But, ah, the intermingling.

1942

Saturday, 7 November
The taste of life is nasty in my mouth. I walk the street passing shadows in the partial blackout. All are seeking, what, they, we, know not. Some, surcease from passion's pricking and all for relief from loneliness and lack and loss. One feels Fate's hand sweeping indiscriminate. Walking with eternal calmness on through the shadows, I meet a fine, stalwart, clean type, young M.P. and a strange, electric something thrills between us but we pass pretending to be unmindful of it. Darker shadows. Blackout. One wants to scream and run. Not for the darkness. No! but for the long arm of Evil with clawing fingers stretched from Europe and from the whole theatre of actual combat for it reaches where we walk. Un-bombed.
"Hi, baby!" you walk on and hear no more of him.
"Goin' my way, beautiful?" you pass on and he fades from sound. Tobacco smell. Body smell. Food smell. Motor horns. Newsboys. Singing drunks.
How hard so many women find it that the father of the babes in their wombs have died.
What of women whose husbands-to-be are never-to-be?
What of the dream babies never to be born? Oh, the voice of their weeping is but a strangled cry in their (our) throats.
What of those of us who dare not lie down to weep for that we would not have the strength to rise again?
Oh, the generations that will remain unborn. We cry out against rapine but Nature determines that children *will* be born *somehow* they are.

Why?

My thoughts go
Round and round
Tumbling over themselves
Madness nudges me
Love one roiling wave of pain
Uncontrollable
God! I cry
Why? Why!

Essential Me

My Essential Me is dainty of foot, tall, lithe, slim-curved
A willow in the wind of Love
A flame, one with the Flame of Life, cognizant of things
Unseen, attuned to the Unheard, Atavistic, Prophetic,
Spanning distance by Spiritual Force, Seeing that not
Present
Receiving intended and unintended Thought-
Vibrations
Grasps hands with God-Life-Force and
As the airborne lifts on a thrust of provided power.
The fullness of the Universe is mine,
I, in it, it in Me.

Exchange

I would exchange my rhyming lines for
the symmetry of new-washed clothes
to hang and blow with mine
on a backyard line.
For the typewriter rather
the sound of the washing machine.

For arms full of files, would joyfully
gather a babe to my breast,
and glad rags, unsoiled, a lap spilled
with the living of children
have them crawl and climb over me
Cooing, crying, touching me
With wee, soft love-strong hands
For empty-handed I.

The Wolf-Dog . . .

I see a black, long, lean, hungry wolf-dog
The lines of its body are ugly
Against the white road
In its nasty potential is
Lust the same.
I need a battle song to stir my blood
To martial feeling and whip my determination
To a white heat
Ah! The face Lust wears is fair.

Mating

What mate can mate me save one with Ink
In his veins? I found Him! I lost Him!
For blood was overcome of Ink.
Why did you not grow red also, O, Ink!
For without Him, would you not bear smaller fruit.
Yet, I suspect you of dealing me a harsh blow
For your gain. You knew, when I did not,
That Sorrow of him not Satisfaction
Would overflow to my Pen.

Toes

When your toes do
Jig and jag
Fast and free
On the knee
Up to see
Tip and toe
Bending low
High and higher
Low and lower
High and higher
Low and lower
Sides do shake
Bend the waist
Fling the tresses
Swing the dresses
O, me
Tweedly-deedly-dee-dee-dee!

No More

No more finagling
God does not want for me
What I want
Dare I contest
Would war with
Mighty Archangel Michael
Whose would the wounds be
Dare I combat majesty?

Why not bow to contain
My good spirit?
My soul's torments
Breed my body's pains.
Sometimes we battle
Our own selves
For
Or
Against our own soul
We must not lose
Yet
With Archangel Michael
We dare think to win
And by winning,
Lose . . .

Question

Is there a woman
Never violated, never demeaned
Never incest-slain
Never by man inflicted pain?

Pain

Times, I invite a new pain
To conquer the unbearable
times, I grasp at sight at sound:
A saw on wood
Roll of car
Beat of horse's hooves—anything to beat louder
Than hammering pulses of pain,
Pain. Pain.

Pain vibrates thru me
Electro-magnet-ic-ally
Why does the world
Sing,
Sing, in praise of love?

Which

Poetry sings a sad song
Or a glad song
Of victory
Or despair
Flings its music on the air
On the mountain
In the valley
Singing. Singing. Singing.
Do You hear?

She

Diaphanous
The blue
That floats about her
Beauty encompassing
Beauteous things
Beauty giving beauty wings.

My Mother . . .

Even Death bowed to her . . .
Softly, yes, only the touch of a loving finger as on a babe's cheek.
With love even, Death bowed to take her. Saluting her life-long voyage: strange steel, cuirassed about one so gentle.
She met All with forward march. Bravely, she went to meet the Dread One, vanquish his power and strangeness, warming his heart.
Softly, in her sleep he took her . . . just a touch upon her cheek he was. Yes, but my love also met him for her, with her. He must have smiled in empathy at these two, indomitable.

Smashing

Some, smashing china
Tumbling furniture
Flinging garments
In a wife's or lover anger
'Gainst a man
Not me
Not then
Now
If on a day
When hatred
Of the species male
Should me consume
Should he
At my front door appear
Might I not slash him through
And through
When love to hatred turned?

High Endeavour

And if you can, as warrior
Fling Pain's gauntlet
Back at Fate
And
Lose
And
Laugh
You'll win.

Question

Why do we, you and I
And everyone
Continue to refer to
Me, we, us as Women
As "Mankind?"
When we, you and I
Creators
Nurture womankind and mankind
In *our* psyche
In *our* mind
Within *our* bodies
How then, can Mankind
Mean Womankind?

Ah! Hah!

God-glad
I rose
At morning new
What e'er at night
I had of rue
Was gone.

Artistry

Dedicated to Bruce Wendell at The Organ

No organ stood on stage
Nor breathless folk sat silent
While a mortal there sweet music made.

Ah! No! but 'twas in Faery
That Pan on reed did pipe
And now and then a laughing brook
Did add a tender silvery strain
Titania too, and Oberon their court
Did hold with dance and song anon
And all the people of the woodland fair
With blossom and green fern
In breast and hair
The melody of their laughter gave
To the enchanted air.

Then martial drum and warriors' feet
Came tramping down my dreamland's street.

And as your organ sang, it sang to me
Of Picardy and Samarkand. Araby and Mantua
Forli, Florence, Padua,
Lorenzo and his Jessica, Juliet and Romeo
O'Overture and Paul Dunbar.

But, Ah, you ceased.
In memory now, my soul repeats
That glimpse of immortality.

For You

I reach my hands
Out into the vibrations
Of the Past
I pluck what I desire
Here,
I present it to you.

The News

It is one o'clock News
What does time mean to me?
Whether it is going or staying
What if it stopped now
What matter?

Faith

Waves of sung faith
Strong supporting 'round me
Church is a place
For crying and loving
And singing and joying
Praying and
Comforting
Loving and giving
For releasing and receiving
In song and prayer
Floats every other heart's salvation.

Euphoria

Euphoria ripples through me
Like a scented wind
No why needed
Love and health
And power and glory
The rightness of things
Fate brushed aside
God's psychological moment
On angel's wings
All my desires fulfilled
In the joy the morning brings.

Death

I planted the seed of a dream
Deep in the soil of my soul.
I watered my dream with Hope's gentle rain
And prayed that the seedling would grow
Tall, green-leaved and strong,
Budding blossoming, and in the happiest moment
Bearing fruit, luscious and ripe.
Hope's life-giving rain has ceased
And the flood of my tears, salted with sorrow
And acid with bitterness have killed the tender leaves
And black is the tree of my dreams.
Only a dry, dead stalk marks the spot like a gravestone
Where my dream once grew.

Desire

Comes a time, when naught suffices
Save the thing desired.
Toil is no panacea, possessions no pleasure
Prayer is a question mark, hope a deferment
God seems asleep.
Quieted my laughter, weary my soul to death
Spiritless I,
To some mazy, dust-fogged cavern
Of grey weariness my soul
would crawl in
Cinder-small to die.

Fear–Why

Evening and the early hours of night
Hold enchantment.
But, at midnight, I must off to bed
The retreating clamour of the longest hour
Sinks in thick depths of after-silence and
I strain my ears for companionship of sounds.
The wind is silent as so animal and human life.
I still seek and crave some littlest sign of living
For I am afeard that mine should be the only waking heartbeat.
I hear a whistling breath, listen again for it
Only to find it is mine own. The window rattles fearfully
Malevolently-minded?
I rise stiffly and softly from my window seat
Fear prickling my back for the malevolent Might-be.
Someone—a brother, with solid human feet enters
And I forget the weird after-midnight fears, climb into bed and sleep.

Symmetry

The symmetry of a flower
In my hand
I
Hold
Admiring.

Just Asking

One day, or was it
night;
"God, have you ever used a computer?"
"Yes, my child, The Universe!"

Charming

She'd toss over her shoulder
Her glorious hair
Imperiously, charmingly
With a smile and a wink
But don't you think
You
Can cheeky be
Or
She'd lose her charmingly.

Multum in Parvo

My Mind
Blest with power
Gathering knowledge
Moment by moment
Hour by hour.

Woman

To be a woman
Is to inherit
Dark memories.

Chip Chop

Hold me. Never let me go!
"No. No."
"Go. Go."
"Yes. No."

Intrusion

I sit in church
Worshipping
Ecstatic in song
The flesh intruding.

Praise

I have had the urge to praise God recently—praise for
The New Year and Christmas before that; thankful praise
for Mahalia Jackson and for Barbara Streisand
And the wealth of Friendship,
For wind and rain and the end of Sorrow, for codfish
and potatoes, for turkey, for the people that make up my day:
My ferry pilot and the boatmen over hundreds of safe
journeys, for the gulls that swoop and dance and soar in
wind and water ballet, for the foam and gale they glory in.
For silences and excitement, striving and rest. For an empty
purse that so quickly fills up and stretches miraculously
when I strive to be unselfish.
Praise for the benevolence of sunshine in the morning's
promise and the deep, delightful softness of rest. For the
surge of Christmas goodwill from strangers and the
thoughtfulness of those we already know . . . for the reminder
that, if I praise with my every breath, yet will I lack to fully
thank Thee. Thou Creator of All Things. So, for My love
I give Thee mine, and strive
To make it nearer Thine.

There

Weary, thirsty, in despair
I came to a green and leafy glade
Cool and sweet as Jesus' breath

About to Go Away . . .

I look upon Home now as doubly dear knowing
I am about to leave it.
It is a haven, a walled-off sanctified heaven surrounded by storms and evils endured by others, itself invulnerable. Our storms, quickly forgotten disagreements and wranglings do not spoil it—only contrast it more vividly:

The nursing kitten. Mother at the oven peering at half-baked delights. Small One rapturously licking the mixing bowl spoon. I stand and cherish them for tomorrow's memory in a far country.

"Boys, stop skylarkin', you'll break those glasses," mildly, Mom admonishes.
The noise is always unchecked—scream or stomp as you please. Oh, joy!

The house is empty as I come home from work. They've all gone to a picnic. The rooms are sad. The quiet and prolonged tidy-ness are strange.

How glad I am to see them go. How much more glad to see them back.

It is not easy to say to them all: "I love you, you who are mine." I leave it unsaid save by my heart, or at Mother's Day, or Christmas, or by some small impulsive act
shying away from the words.

Womb Time

Into the womb of night
I go
Back to Mother
As embryo.

Voyager

My spirit leaps wildly and with beautiful energy
in my body, protesting its cage, beating against the sides.
Has stretch beyond it, yet, will not
An' I lose it and the animal body lose balance.

I lay smiling into space. Walt Whitman, that early-born
Modern had written for me the "Untold Want."
"The untold want, by life and land ne'er granted.
Now, Voyager, sail forth to seek and find."

I smiled into space at the vast beauties the words
Depicted. Smiled to visualize that success but
Waits for me to achieve it. Smiled till it seemed foolish
To smile. My eyes and my cheeks smiled
My heart laughed and bubbled till my laughter broke forth.
Sweetness overflowed me as milk flows from the soft half
globe of a mother breast.
Life but awaits my voyaging
I must always after the intangible.
If I but catch the sweet of its breath I must have
That fraction's sweetness than staid un-inspiration.

Why I Believe

Having foolishly gone to a lonely spot
With a man I knew little about—
Women often question their sanity later than the fact—

"God help me!" I prayed.
Around the corner ran a group of children
Chasing a ball.

Lucifer

Once, I
In evil case
Medusa-like
Appeared, my hair unkempt
From ocean-salt
I only knew
From my friend's hand swift-crossing
Of her breast
The Satan in my face
For I had pushed aside
For evil's pleasure
My soul's good place

Where do souls reside
When Evil pushes them aside?

Impeccable

To the female eye
Impeccable tail-or-ing
Draws like a magnet
And sets everything vibrating
Implies impeccable all will be.

Daylight Saving

When the clocks they forward turned
Time, they say is early.
And now since clocks they backward turn
Time, they say is right.
Make no mistake, its Time retains
Its measured ways
No matter what the pundits sayed.

Wings

The birds soared out of the dawn-bright East.
Higher, the Warplanes zoomed but the birds floated
downwind, quietly, un-business-like
Joie-de-vivre, sweet with health surged thru her.
While she stretched
for the feel of muscle and curve, fluid or taut.
A great strength, a quiet force, not her own,
yet within her took charge
She,
With the birds not war.

The Funeral

The silence accents solemnity
The muted organ commences its affirmation
The funeral bell insists the presence of death. The glorious stained glass windows lift the ache.
The blue-backed hymnals and red-covered prayer books
Challenge the coffee-brown pews.
The slow file of mourners enters the church
Moving in their separate sorrows
To pass the open casket for one last beloved look.

The widow's veiled face is frozen with contained grief.
The son is more moved than the daughter, the cousin than the granddaughter.

The resonant promise of "I am the Resurrection and the Life," of the intoning Anglican clergyman has given way to the comfort of the 23rd Psalm. The hodge-podge choir is of little assistance to the congregation in the vaulted cathedral.

A sob breaks from someone, while all the rest hold fast to their control because of it. As the eulogy is given, each work a true one, idiosyncrasies included, hearts lift. For each sings a song of triumph describing a soul that lived and died unperturbed.
The minister talks of death as a "Home-going."

We Girls Talkin'

She and I agree
As far as she and I are concerned
A woman is a fool
Who does
A woman is a fool
Who doesn't.
What choice do we have?

One of Us:
"He told me I wouldn't see his heels for dust."

Another One:
"How many of them loved you?"
"None, I guess."
"You sure didn't love them."

An Older:
"For nigh forty years gone by
I still desire Him who never *had* me.
Of course, that's because I'm the fool
That didn't, don't you see?"

Older Still:
"You see, I know about how men think about women,
you and me.
Oftimes, when man wants a piece, he sometimes wants a
piece besides the piece, he wants a piece of property
And that's how I figured it out to be:
Now, you see, after that
He said to me
'I don't want you to think it's
because of your property.'
Me, silently: 'Tee hee!'"

"Just about then I found out
about the wife, you see.
(he don't know about that)
Tee hee! Tee hee!
And just *then* he said to me
'Won't you sell to me your property?'
That was for just about $100,000
Less than it out to be!
Tee hee! Tee hee! Tee hee!"

"So, you see lotsa times a man wants a *piece*
He also intends to be given the piece of property
Well he didn't get a *piece*."

"And that's why he didn't get a piece of my property.
Tee hee! Tee hee! Tee hee! Tee hee!
Besides, I don't think even a good husband should get that
piece of we girls' property.
The days of primogeniture are dead. Don't you see?"

Woman

Some are pretty. Some are beautiful
Few are lovely—
She was . . . I had to restrain myself
From confronting her with—
"Lady, your walk disastrous contrast
To your beauty!"

Another . . . She was the tweedy type
Clothes
A walking stick even
Yet, she all but
Floated
By me.

Yet Another . . . She was a farm woman
Standing at the bus stop
Erect. Regal even.

One more . . . Grandmamma
Walking
She was a tall ship
In full sail.

Today's female hustling by
in pants
Keeping up with the hi-tech male
Standing.
Legs spread wide
The graceful woman
Went out with the crinoline.

Music

Get-in-your-bones
Tickle-your-toes-music
I mean really—O, love me darling
Hug me Sweet
Put your arms around me Honey
The big bass fiddle
Twing, twang, twining
maracas zoom, zeem, zoom
Zoom, zooms, zoom zooms
zoom.
More than one fate is tuggin'me
The sweet Now and the Unanswered To Be
Tico, tico-ticklin' honeeeey.

Peace

All along my length I am a prayer . . .
My toes that touch the floor, my knees
That bend, my body curved to couch,
My elbows, arms, my head that bends
To my supplicating fingers.
All of all of me thrills
With peace toward God
For the needs of those I love
For the deeds of those who hate

How?

There are fearsome questions,
Am I really me?
How did I come to be?
Can love unlock the mystery?

Ocean

The ocean is my mother
The ocean is my father
The ocean is my beginning
Yet
It will not be the end of me.

I had eyes to see . . .

Lovers

Their joy permeated everywhere
The flowers flung censers of perfume
The zephyrs swayed the grasses
The sun enfolded all.
Those lovers were one with the universe,
Breathing in the scent of blossoms,
Singing with the trill of birds
Dancing with the blown grasses,
Laughing in each other's eyes.

Being

I am a sounding board
For the emotions of the Universe.
Melody or Dissonance
They vibrate from me.

Sly

Temptation assails in so many ways
Slimy ways and intricate.
Temptation comes and knocks, and, after being booted out,
Comes back, and slyly whispers.
"Why not yield to me now
Then, all yearning will be done
You will be free of insistence
Hereafter,
I promise."
"Ha! Ha! Ha! Then one will be securely bound
With bands like hoops of steel, bands that bite
Into the very soul
But I will not."
I have fought some royal battles
And achieved some royal victories
And will?

Sunday 24 March, 1968

Not only do I reach out
Scooping up Infinity
From the stream of things—
I impact the stream of things
With my Essence.

Votive

Each dawn I seek
A handful of achievements
To offer votive to night

Difference

God, in miracles
Bypasses
What we believe
Is
Natural law.

Poetry

Poetry is
The daughter
Of Joy
And
The mother of Sorrow.

Ain't It

Ain't the one
Who is not The One
Better
Than no-one?

Men

Men! MEN! MEN!
penises—
All's got 'em
All that power.

Yes

Of all the gifts
That God has given
Songs a foretaste are.
Are of Heaven.

Ha! Hee!

I sit, prissy quiet, sipping tea
Meantime . . .
Desire rip-roars through me.

Fate Pain

When we decide to hit out at Life
It's We we hit
not it.

True

"The evil men do lives after them"
And e'en from the grave
Impels destructively

Birth

I witnessed birth today
By a yellow flower acacia tree
Where I happened to be
A chrysalis next to me
Emerged butterfly
Instantly
Yellow as could be
Alighting exactly on
The Yellow flower on that tree.

The Blueprint

My soul is in the deep darkness my subconsciousness lies
weeping
I limp within myself
Joy is only a surface thing, the clown's mask
Yet, the blindness of immaturity
Must yield to the gouge of anguish
And
God-sculpted, the Real Me
Begins to take shape like the Infinite Blueprint.

VOLUME II

Love Songs & Songs of Love

Love Songs

Us

Of

Two

The

From: Both of Us

These . . . me to you

You

You are more beautiful to me
than the sun that rises
after a night of pain.

You to me are taller
than the palm tree of the valley
that rises to meet the sun

Your countenance is lovelier
than "A cluster of camphire
in the vineyards of Engedi."

You, my Beloved, are the vision of
mine own soul
clothed and laughing, playing
and praying and leaping, running
and loving and sleeping and crying
and meeting I and thee
In We.

All Green Things

All green things growing
Are ways of saying, ways of showing
I love you
As I pass them I recall you
Know you, show you all the
Welling, swelling, filling
Love of you.

When you walk this way, they'll sing it
Show it, laugh it, bring its message
Shining green and fragrant
Love you, love you.
Love you, love you.

Dark greens, bright greens, light greens, fine ones
Huge trees, small ones, lacy fern'ry
Stauncher creepers, Mexican sleepers,
Fruit greens, apples, cherries.

Reds and purples, crimsons, lavenders
Flash of redbirds, flaming sunsets
Patterns, posies and my red lips

Blues of sky and ocean near us
Sinking sun and stars moon rising
Shone above my blue eyes
Gazing in your brown ones.
We partook of God's divineness

Silvers, gold we speak of
Under silver beauty moon-gold.
When the dying sun's rays linger
As they leave the sky moon goldens
Glows with fire 'gainst black night-time
So our love with this world's background.

I would rise in might and power
Fly to heaven
Sweep and swoop o'er all horizons
Cry with loud cries thun'drous music
See and know all things immortal
Yet,
'Twere not enough to love you
Show you how I love you.

Yet, the marvel of the knowledge
that to you all things of beauty I am—
Light and fragrance glory, honour,
Mercy, kindness, wisdom, softness
Earth things, heavenly, fills me
Permeates, surrounds me
With a peaceful, tumbling glory.

Love you. Love you.

Rhapsody

Your being is like a Rhapsody
Played by the hand of God for me.
Now glory as from violin strings
Sweep forth from you on tender wings
Now quickly as from a harp
A quiver softly sad is heard
'Tis when a child has kissed your face
With all its tender infant grace.
And now, Beloved, organ tones
Forth from your soul in grandeur roll
'Tis when a kindness has been done
With heart on fire for glory won
Then soft, again, Ah! Softly soft
Like music from the Christ child's heart
When then at night thou goest to rest
In faith reclining on thy Saviour's breast.

All

You are the sparkle
On sunlit waters
You are the cresting
Of a running sea
You are the bird flight
From dawn time rising
You are all of Life to me.

In Silver Slowness

In silver slowness, the sea-wind climbs the ocean's back.
A little zephyr sets rivulets to run among the palms.
Casuarina furze is hung with bright fruit of stars.
Piled snow are the clouds on the horizon's lip.
The globed moon last night was full.
You approach and the winged stars start from their places
Hastening earthward they fire me where I stand
They?
'Tis You have lighted me! It is with You I burn!

Seeds of Content

Silver sails a-slumbering in a calm lagoon.
Fairy stars a-trembling 'neath a silver moon.
Golden clouds a-showing how the day-dead sun
Still as subjects numbers
The cloudlets one by one
Tranced lovers drifting in heaven-bright ecstasy
Love! The gods are mating the hearts of You and Me.

Thorns

On the
Strings of my heart
Ecstasy and
Agony
Both
Which one to die on?

I sing of love
I sing of glory
I sing the pain
I sing the sadness
Of all who lie
Love-slain.
When the Rose of Love
Has died
'Tis the thorns remain.

If

If I had known
that love would be
the death of me
would ever loved?
Yet
Can it be
That
Agony
Is born
Of
Ecstasy?

Come

O Love, sweet love come
Come.
The moon is high and the dark trees
Throw their wind-tost shadows
On the moon-washed
And
My heart awaits you
Oh, come.

If

If you should come and call tonight
I would arise and go.
If it were dark without one light
I would arise and go.
If you were old and crippled and blind
I would arise and go.
Or sad or hard or strange
You'd find
I will arise and go.

Beyond

I love you beyond thought and thinking
Beyond singing and sighing and saying
Beyond tears and agony
Beyond my hope of Eternity.

If God should will you die
Before me
That would be my gift
To save you agony.

Becoming

With overflow of love
I am become
a violin
sweet and wailing
an organ
thunderous and rolling
Drums
Making such a joyful noise
A soprano, tenor soaring
I
Invading Heaven's gate
Loving, loving, loving.

Never

I would soar upward
Clasp the stars
A diadem for your brow
Flowers from a thousand gardens
a carpet for your feet.
Pile up all the loves
Of all times and climes
To embrace your fine-liness.
Never was a love like ours
Past, present or future even
For our love
Is earthly Heaven.

The Sword

The sword of Sorrow shreds my heart
By love's own hand.
I never thought that love
Would be the death of me.

More

The night leaps live
At your approach
The scent of flowers enter my pores.
The golden moon warms me
the stars burn within me
All this that I write
Is insufficient small and unworthy.

Nothing that I write
Is half as beautiful
As your own words to me.
It is so sweet
That you should feel
That what you write
Is not enough
For still I gain
As you write more
And more and more.

Eternity

As the petals of a blossom
Unclose in the morn of Spring
So my heart opens
At your touch of love.
In purity, eagerly
In passion, slowly.

If Only

An' my Love were here
We would wing hand in
Close-clasped hand
Out, over the ocean
Over the sea
Higher and higher
In ecstasy rising
Sail by the moon
To thread our way side
By side
The stars
To ride the sun's
Morning chariot
My love and I,
kissed by dawning's dew
Plunge into the sea's wave
Riding the breakers
Joining the bluebird
In the air
We, each dissolving self
Become one.

Twins

Love wields twin swords
Si-mul-taneous-ly
Pain embracing Ecstasy.

Passion

The moon is bright
And I sway my body pliant
Upwards
I lift my face
And send my heart's call
Out and far away
To the heart of my life.
O pain of me, blood of me
Bone of me, pulse
Feel my heart's call across the night.
I tell each star of heaven my yearning
Beg them tell thee how I love Thee—
See them Darling, see them burn
With my passion the brighter.

Variety

I love thee madly
with a sweet content
I love thee calmly
with a wild lament
Joy shapes it
Beauty makes it
Sleep holds it
Dawn folds it
Day molds it
My love.

Tyrant

Love is a cruel tyrant
It keeps me in its thrall
Love is a cruel tyrant
Demands from me my all
What does it have for me?

We Two

On a sudden I look up from my bookkeeping
And laugh into a mirror and murmur, while joy shivers thru me
"I love you." My heart says it, sings it.
What matter that my lover may be
Ten thousand land, or air, or miles of sea away from me—
heart-close we'll always be.

Wondering

My heart is naked before you
With only our souls mating
Our bodies so long apart
I suffocate with need of you
Need to express our love.
I wonder with a great despairful wonder
Will we mate in Paradise?

Fate

We thumb our nose
At Fate
The universe a ball
Our littlest finger
Arrogantly
to twist
no sorrow
dare come near us.

Entire

I send you all my soul
With me remains
Ex-cru-ci-a-ting-ly
Love's pains
Pains! Pains! Pains!

You

Safe in
Fantasy
You
Deny me
Reality . . .
As I cannot have you
Deny me not my dream.

Hiding

On, on I go
In anguished woe
Love hides from me
behind each tree
Calling, calling, calling.
Thus, it maybe,
my travels never done
will be.

Caged

The wings of a great sad need
Beat with slow ceaselessness
Against
The cage that is my life.
The winged beat forever
Beats
With my wants caged within
Love
It
Is imprisoning me.

Counterpane

Parted are we
Yet
The wings of sleep
Love's counterpane
Will be.

Alone

I dare not dream.
I dare not let my poor heart flood with love
When songs are sung
When dawn grows bright or daylight fades.
Nor can I take kind Hope to bed with me.
Nor can the Dawn hold out a promise.
Every time these come nigh, I must shut the door
To shut them out—for it is they compound this
Ceaseless circle of my heart pain
Compounded by unending pain of memory
While a-leap with Life, alone. Alone. Alone am I
Alone.

For Me

With slow, effortless grace
A bird flew above me
More like butterfly than bird
Wheeling, soaring in widening circles
Higher and higher away from me
I near swooned with delight to see it
I hold my breath as it goes out of sight
Smiling at the memory
Bird that flew for me
Thou and I
Comprehend Eternity.

Euphoria

I am in an opera mood tonight. My soul could swing on the high trapeze of an aria out into the infinite, circle the world on mountaintops of song. My own or another's music could melt me into every note, each pore of me could throb song a-pulse with ecstasy.

Fling the sad carcass of the physical aside. Shed the material. Love on the spiritual heights.
Give breath and breadth to the soul to rise and soar upward
Un-encumbered. Then would it be strung as a silver
bracelet the world around.
With song, then, become all Soul to listen.

Sonnetry

I would write a sonnet
In praise of my beloved.
People would believe
I praised Zeus himself
Mt. Olympus is found
Wherever my Beloved
Sets his feet.
Never was man or god
Like unto him.
All Nature is embryonic
In his stature
And accomplishment.
There is none like him now
Or ever will be.

Encompassing

We walk our love
We talk our love
We smile and sing it.
I melt at your approach
Time holds its breath
The world about fades away
The while our souls embrace.

Exultant

Spirit-gathered
Half a century
Of sublimated woe and ecstasy
Joy and agony of love.
So sighs my song
Up from my heart
'round the moment dancing
Gathering up my Beloved.

Parted, yes, together
Tele-path-ically
Ensures our soul's embrace
Gathering up my Beloved

Desire

Desire buffets in great waves
As the ocean; a ship
As I . . .
If You came now . . .

When

When the jasmine blossom
Swings her censor of perfume
I think of You

When songs of love
Or sad or gay
Bring You as two steps away
I dream of You.

When the night bird
Trills unto his mate
I'm wanting you.

When thoughts of You,
Heart of my heart
My pulses very beat
'Tis this I must repeat
My love to You.

Pain

The violins wailing
Tell
The midnight stars
My pain.

Yours

Round words, little ones
with a teasing sound
Turning on the tongue.

Your golden words of love
globed as full moons
Shining.
Luscious of meaning
Succulent, bursting
With passion.

Unending

This never-ending torture
On the rack of Love
Condemned to die endless tomorrows
I live only for the joy in morning's promise.

Why

Why did I fall in love?
That's when the bruising started.
Why can't I turn love off?
What turned it on anyway?
Love's re-christened Tantalus.

Talk

You said
Come, let us sit together
We will talk our whole soul
Thou and I. Yes . . .
And
Underneath
Without within
All-encompassing
Wherever I am, I
With Thee
Thou
in Me
Eternally.

Sold

I know you will not come tonight, and yet I feel
You near. I watch and wait and all whispers of sound
Are your imagined feet.
Just as I am about to turn inside, I see another man
Approaching—he would do for my purpose—any man would do.
All men would do.
I turn inside, cursing myself for a fool.
I *am* a fool . . .
"Love," they say, "is a breach in the wall, a broken gate."
"Love," they say, "sells the proud heart's citadel
to fate."
And I am sold.

Despair

My heart sags . . .

My eyes are down and I notice every seam, bump and depression in my path. I have become aware of one foot going in front of the other automatically. I wonder how long they can. Over the wall the birds are singing Spring. I quicken my pace; take a deep breath, then try again. I should try to buy some starch, starch for my backbone. Where to go to buy? There are others in far worse case than mine. Or is it they put on a better face? The sun is out. My heart flutters like a captive bird weary with beating its wings against inevitability.

Lovers

Lovers laughing in each others' eyes.
My life quivers with pain
In the midst of crowds
I am separate, suffering.
I conceive of others I see happy always
Yet
I hear across the years Anthony, crying
"I am dying, dying, dying, Egypt, dying."
And so I die.

Wine

I'm inclined to drown myself in wine
Bathe in it, pore-absorb it
Eye and hair and ear, nostril and mouth
Slobber my body with it
All orifices, indentations, dimples
To cry, "Wine! Wine! Wine!"
Feet that might have crushed the vine
Cry, "Wine! Wine! Wine!"

Then say: "My Love is Wine,"
Love is Wine.

La Traviata

To see . . .

"La Traviata" the Lost One*—I too,
I too, must I also out into the blackness
Forsaken of Fate of destiny mocked, of Love denied
Of living done?

For I must give You up. Even as Dumas'
"Lady of the Camelias" gave up her
Beloved—but I, I have never had Thee. When thou wast
deeply surely mine I loved another vainly. And Now there
is no depth to now,
No Now of Thee for me.

Yet of sacrifice even I draw a sweet, a hurting
Deep-pained sweet, a dying while forced cruelly
To live to witness my own death.
Out of life would I? Too much unlived to go
this soon.
Love while loving, I have never known—
Love-unloving, Yes, and Loving-unloved
These have been my portion, each and ache.

**Not fallen—lost*

Two

A woman in love
Walks
with a proud grace
And I am proud.

Love-Need

I want! I want! I want! I ache with the sweetness of love pent up. I ache with the need to give. I ache for my lover hard against me. Hard with his own unfathomed ache-ings sore prest with love pent up. Oh, to abandon me! The wind of passion puts its swift moving hand under my loins and sets the blood of my veins to wild movement as the waves of a storm surge lose their own volition. Utterly overcome me, my Love so that my demurs may be feeble. So that my strongest opposing gain nothing but a fierce overpowering. Overpower me with your strong and towering manhood make me weak with a delicious tingling weakness. Then stronger than the concentrated might of an army fiercer than sword thrust take and drink of blood, slake yourself. Give me to drink also. Give and receive at one. Soul of my love . . . Love of my soul give and receive at one.

Recall

Seeing their young, young love
The sheen upon it brought smiles to my heart . . .
Remembering.

Here and There

That I lov'd you so little, Then and so little Now would hold no thinking on save that in the time between I loved so deeply. Cloud froth of joy that had neither body nor words to give it sustenance but thrived on absence and distance bodied by the spirit. That was my youth time, happy was I each organ performed its function perfectly touched by the oil of happiness.

Cherished

The 'kerchief that you proffered for the crying of my tears last night, I cherish now for the essence and substance of You it holds from the breath of your happy, healthy young pores and the cleanness of your loving heart there in this white square. I bury my nose in it and savour all of love animal and spiritual breathing in your outward breath.

Haloes

The love-words I write
Move from their places
Form haloes 'round your head
Knowingly
Lovingly.

Yearning

My heart yearns to You
as the blossom
to the sunlight,
the honey to the bee
Would I were the morning dewdrop
to cup your kiss of love.

Together

Parted. yes, together
Telepathically
Ensures our souls embrace.
"I Love You" a silver ribbon
On a May wind
Or spiked rain-silver from the sky
On me exultant.

You

You
Are my
Intermezzo
Leading onward
To
Our crescendo

Come

O, Love, Sweet love, come.
Come.
The moon is high and the dark trees
Throw their shadows
On the moon-washed roadway.
And
My heart awaits you
Oh, come!

Piling

In the silences
Piling, piling
Love is dying
Dying, dying
While it dies
Its agonies live.

All

All along my length I lie
Desiring you
Intolera-bly

Caro Mio Ben

I would that I might pour out upon You
As the sun pours out its beams
Upon the wide earth.
I wish I were golden and glorious as the sun—
I could cover you with My Love.
Or,
If I were the moon queen in the night sky
I would kiss you in beauty, bewitch you
With my shining, peep at you
Now and again
From behind a cloud and smile at you
As I nestled among the stars.
The Italians say, "Caro mio ben,"
Meaning, "Joy of my heart,"
As thou,
Art
Joy of my heart.

Within

Within this love
I, dying, live
And
Loving, die.

Fire

Fire along our breath
Fire on fire of mouth on mouth
Breast a-breast
Limb along limb
heart thunder 'gainst heart thunder
Throbbing palm on throbbing palm
With lips mutual fire
We lie
Wine whipping through our veins.

Immortal Moment

1960
Laughing, he lifted me, lightly I lay
as the ruffling wind on the sea's back
lay lightly in lithe arms
as running he came
to the edge of the sea.

Twilight blew a golden trumpet
as the sun exploded in glory
and while the slim-curved
silver moon took stage
The stars,
as ladies-in-waiting
appeared.
The firmanent formed the frame
Around our moment of Infinity.

No Release

For half a century
He has never let me go.
Nor does he come to claim me.

Over and over again I say,
"It is over. It is ended.
It is finished. It is done."
It is never over. It is never ended.
It is never finished. It is never done.

Life, Fate mock me
Do they get pleasure
Of my trauma?

Shana

He dug his fingers, clutching softly

within the midnight masses of her
waist-long hair

To the roots probed and pressed
and tugged

Separating strands and masses

of her pride and joy and passionate-ness

At nape and temple
shaping all the rounds and bumps
He tugged

Then stripping, clothed himself
In Shana by her hair

Slowly . . . as a woman hypnotized,
Slowly . . . as a woman dreaming
All her heart and brain a-melting
Slowly . . . as a maid resisteth
knowing she has lost the battle
Meltingly, she languished lovely
Curving to the couch she slaked him
While he clothed himself
In Shana by her hair

("a" in Shana as in "ma.")

Love's If

The moon'd still shine for us
A kind Fate spin for us
And Time stand still for us
If love were all

The stars would fight for us
The heart of night for us
Would ever throb for us
If love were all.

Glory would cling to us
Sorrow would
Fling from us
If love were all.

Anticipation bright
In thy sweet dawning light
Destine for us aright
Let love be all.

Memories

Memories—never to die
Of past blossoming to keep perfume
Laid in the lavender of the years
Moist a thought with tears
Fringed with laughter free and soft
Ah! In prayer I have oft remembered Thee
In prayer remember Me.

Glory Moon

The moon rose, splendid and caressing
You, my love and I, the others apart.
We lay on soft pink sands
With silver-gold petals of the moonflower
Scattering glory upon us, enfolding
Gathering we two one with God's creation
We lie, untouching, no need to embrace
our boundaries the parameter of the Universe.
One with all that Is
And shall be
Enraptured
Within
That once-only
Moonlight.

1981

The tears come slowly
as tho' dissolving from
my whole body
One long head to toe pain
So complete as to be
Ecstasy.

Gently

Gently, gently first, gently
till our souls fuse
Then
Fly off on wings of Ecstasy.

If Only

Flirting on the edge of danger joyfully
We,
One, advancing
One, retreating
Lingering-ly
Tasting sweetness
Wondering, Should we—
What the future be

Best not. Worst not
Torture-lingly
Rapture moment we forfend.
Parents not too far
enough away.

Why
I
Now Condemned
Never, ever knowing
That Magic Moment utterly
Hearing eternally
Only
The muted music of the Might-Have-Been.

Then

When the dawn birds wake and sing
When the earth is bursting Spring
Then within my heart I sing
I love you.

Higher

I can laugh crazily
Scream or weep
Wanting you, wanting you
O God! O God! Oh
The flames of my desire
Leap higher
If I should sleep
Awaking
Higher leap
The flames of my desire.

Ache

The day is gold and green and blue
And I love you.
I draw my breath to breathe in You.
My every pore a concentrated ache
Of needing You.

All in All

Each pore pouring all within without
Being unto being pressing, kissing
Intermingling

Soul-Genetic

Mine and his genetic nuclei
Have
Born us, soul-twins.

Remember!

To want of body
Love's assurance
Of lack
To other turns.

Drums

Drums
making such a joyful noise
A soprano, tenor soaring
I,
Invading heaven's gate
Loving, loving, loving.

Death

If I were dying
You *would* come
I know, I know.
Should I wish God
To hurry it
That It could then
Be so?

Now. Now

The violins sing of love
Of love's delight
Come, Love. Come
Across the magic night.

Lust

Lust is a tiger
A shark
These teeth bite deep.

Ecstasy

Your love-song
Tossed
Ecstasy
My soul
To catch.

Lost

Could Nepenthe's waters
Drown my sorrows
Would it drown me also?

Question

Why does the God of Love
Deny me
Being loved?
There is thun'drous silence.

So Long

With a great surge of love and need
I commence to sing
Only to find tears choke off my song
O, my God, my Love. You are so long away.

Hate

Love, love, love
With lonely pillow
Now!
To balance Fate I hate, hate, hate.

Would

For a moment's Ecstasy
Would
Forfend Eternity

Both

The tenor, soaring
to crescendo rising
His love-song
sobbing, dying
Mine too,
Sobbing. Dying.

Cherries

I suck the cherry ripeness
Of your mouth.
Sweeter is it than soft winds
Sweetly from the South
Richer is it than red wine
From grapes of Italy
Sweeter, richer than each of these
Is your mouth to me.

Come

The violins sing of love
Of love's delight
Come Love, come
Across the magic night.

Denied

You,
Safe in Fantasy
Deny me
Reality.

Agony

I die for
Love
live
only
hand in hand with
Agony.

Sanctified

This love by Chastity
Sanctified
Yet body yearns
To feast
As others do
Why should I
Be denied?

Even Away

I scent you along my arms
I feel you at my mouth
And taste
I breathe you in the core of me
As Solomon in his Song of Songs
You are as a cluster of camphire
"In the vineyards of Engedi."

VOLUME III

Songs All Around

Impact

To the Soul of the World
For a Fusion of Spiritual force
The August Soviet Czech Invasion

September 26, 1968
Why should not the whole sympathetic world
be gathering up its combined spiritual force
in prayer for Czechoslovakia?
Arms we are not sending
Prayer is our weapon.

In their cage of oppression
They gaze through their bars
Their spirit free
And we
We stand and watch as city crowds
Watch a rapist, a murderer
Lifting no finger to stem
The tide Evil.

If religion has any power
In us—NOW NOW
Must we raise
And rouse us from moral sleep.
Weep? No!
Pray!

January 19, 1969
War being fought without arms
One—against all the might of Moscow
Jan engaged no tanks, no guns,
No Air Force, Army or Navy
Not one soldier did he engage

Yet won.
Proving the spirit mightier than all.
Pallach's fire of self-sacrifice
Leaps red before my eyes
His ever-living spirit
Feeds eternal fuel to his gift-fire
Of martyrdom.

This poem struggles for birth
I am in travail all day . . .
Link me, link me fate with a suffering Czech
Waters that bear this poem-child break—
It *must* be born!

Let us send a wave of vibrating soul-thought
cascading, showering, burning across the air miles
shattering the barriers of opposing force,
The intangible of a man's spirit
Will not be ground into the earth—
Ours the reinforcements.
Vibrate strength of our spirit
Bombard this threatening destruction
Of not Czech'slovakia alone
But all that impinges on Soviet
Cold calculation of de-souled man.

August 1969 . . . From *within* the Soviet camp
Reinforcement comes
A. Kuznetsov, A. Anatol becomes.

Shine words Glow Burn Urge
Motivate Consolidate
Until rank on rank spirit forces
Push Pile Link Multiply
Undefeatable.
Feel us link you. Czechs
Feel us telepath you strength

This should ache us so
This should intertwine us so
Catch us in so strong a heart-trap
That we rise in singing chant forward.
The everyday man is a powerful fellow
Numerically strong: he can raise
A mighty song
His feet can pound a heavy solid
Beat of march.

"There's not a breathing
of the common wind that will forget thee
Thou hast great allies:
Thy friends are exultations, agonies
And love. And man's unconquerable mind."

—William Wordsworth of Toussaitn L'Ouverture

Time Travel

I saw her on the bus . . .
Hers was a Mediterranean face, old ivory
Smooth of check, perfect of line
Her eyes held ancient mysteries, her neck pure Nefertiti
Slowly . . . she turned
Aware of today.

How could I know her?
She is my sister, for I was born in Greece
Five thousand years ago.

How do I know?
When I saw in Realites, the crystal sparkling
Glory of that Grecian air
I rise up exclaiming, "I know *that* house, for I was *there*
Yes, I was also where "Rose-red Petra half as old
As Time" was
For am I not always?

Love

The splendid tints of sky are mine
The boundlessness of sea
The majesty of hills is mine
But I, I seek for Thee

What matters golden of morn
What of the roll of Time
What of all beauty, when I,
Forlorn, find not Thy hand in mine.

When I Began

That atavistic ancestor whose footfall matched the music
that he made as he marched in rhythm with his desire
to reach the far mountain.
The streams that he followed gave him new patterns of song;
the blowing grasses gave his body new bendings
whether in the wind of yearning or of favoring force.
The cats that leaped sinuous in the distance
sent ripples of lithe reaction
through sinews that learned to swim
the ripples of the ever-flowing waters
Now, is all that rhythm mine
bequeathed through the ever living umbilical cord.
They are my subconscious
Unreleased . . . Yes, unreleased
Until Ego-maturity turns the key.

(First published in *Sparrowgrass Voices of America,* 1994.)

Reminder

When the glory of that glittering Grecian sunlight
Bathed me
I was reminded of my own Atlantic Bermuda Island's
Glistening sunlight embracing me.

Date with the Past

Italy . . . In Roman sandals, I,
Where ancient Roman feet once trod
Have trod, O yes, the Appian Way
Where Caesar's legions rolled
And I have stood where Christians died
One hundred thousand souls

And I have breathed in modern
Time
Where ancients breathed before
In Seven-hilled Rome
And sea-girded shore.

And I have walked where Peter fled Domine
"Quo Vadis?" crying
And I have seen where Pope John
Blest the world before his dying
And heard the immortal "Ave"
Ever sweet in cathedral vast up-rise
And seen spires, columns, fountains,
Colonnades,
That everywhere pierce Italian skies.

And I have wandered where
Now dwell the poets, sculptors, painters vying
With Leonardo the great da Vinci
And Michelangelo, the undying.

These Things I Love

Gold pools of sunlight on tree-shaded grass
Hilltop sky at eventide
The siren-call of wide horizons
The mind and hand of my Friend
The intimacies of Silence
Surcease after Pain and
Peace that comes for Faith.

These things I love—
Green grass growing, knowing that the
Bud will further beauty bear
Sleep's resurrecting power
The smile of a passing stranger
The miracle of birth
My mother's infrequent mirth
Her unselfish hands.

I love—
Lights at night, splendid in the dark
And hidden worth in folk whom men
Have called defiled
An infant smiling in its rosy sleep
A poet's placing of the string of words,
Like pearl and amethyst upon a golden chain
Close-clasped 'round Beauty's throat
Rest after travail, sunlight after rain
Night after day, then rosy dawn again.

Nature

Do you smile tenderly because leaves are green
When Spring is new?
Or, softly, because waters run cool, calm and blue?
Does a robin's sweet note and his rich, red throat
Catch at your heart with wonder?
Does a lizard puffing his orange ball
As he sits
On the moss on an old gray wall
Speak to your soul of eternal things.
Bring to your mind other dear, dead Springs.
Bring to life a pure intent
Bring a wish for its betterment?
O, Nature, it is true,
All hearts are touched by you.

(First published in *World's Fair Anthology of Verse,* 1940.)

Flight

Dawn zephyrs* blow across the sky
And touch the face of glory
With kisses rare and soft and sweet
As any told in story.

My thoughts as zephyrs lightly dance
Yet reach the gates of splendour
'Tis then Mortality. Eternity before
Me bow surrender.

(**Zephyrs* became the name of the 1937 book, *Collection of Poetic Thought*.
"Flight" was composed in late teens.)

Firenze

Florentine our Guide was
Steeped in Roman lore
Classic the poetry of that ancient shore
Towering the mountains
Verdant grow the valleys
Wide are the piazzas
Narrow are the alleys

Always the song rises
Ever bloom the flowers
Beauty-laden ever
The enchanted hours.

The Muse

1940
I drank the god's Olympian wine,
And with the Muse I sat entwined
Sipping of her crimson lips
Tasting Paradise in each sip.
Ah! Such joy in my soul did grow
When the Muse I'd come to know.

(First published in *World's Fair Anthology of Verse,* 1940.)

Daughter

Daughter of the wind
Daughter of the sun
And of the sea
Hair flowing free
Limbs riding the wind
She goes
Exultantly

1997

31 August–6 September
from
BERMUDA
To
The British People
The Arabs
The French
The World

Princess Di

The world's in tears
And so am I
All of us for Princess Di
The good she's done
Will live for aye
That's Princess Di.

And now our thoughts
to her sons we turn
let's pray for them
While their hears burn.
Let's follow them
Lovingly.

Not like the Paparazzi.
In life, Princess Di
Embraced the world
Perhaps now, her legacy
Could preserve the monarchy.

Whence

I saw them in the City
Tall, commanding, kingly even
they strode as men of power.

From another plane?
Reincarnated Romans?
One was brown, one was white.
Something in me said:
These men are lovers.
A David and a Jonathan?
Possibly.

The Storm

Arlene
1963

Bending and writhing
Tossing and heaving
Cracking and rending
The trees in the storm

Flattening and shivering
Heightening, dividing
The trees in this storm.

The Storm

Fabian
2003

Crying and pleading
Whistling and speeding
High, low
Far below
The trees in this storm.

Leaping as a wounded insane beast
This monster Fabian
Screaming and picking lashing and slashing
Cutting and butting
Spanking and flogging
Sawing and splitting
Taunting
This miscreant Fabian
When will it cease
When have release
O God, please
No more of this storm Fabian.

I feared for their safety
Those trees in those storms
Then, I quickly remember
The tree that bends, breaks not
And I,
In life's anguish
Bending, praying
will break not
Like trees in life's storms

And, Now
Commiserating, caring
Clearing, cleaning helping
Giving, finding mending
God's help only four loss of life
Back to calm winds calm seas.

The Foam Maiden

The Foam Maiden has dancing silver unpredictable hair
Body of dream, parented by Ocean
In calm water, undisturbed by ship or wind she dies
Ever-reborn, her life is timeless.
Sailing, I glory in her beauty, symmetry and fascination.

The wide, horizon-curving sea is mine.
The day is fine, sun-warmed, zephyr cooled.
Free from care, am I, free from the need to do
Only to be.

See the Sea-born Maiden curling, foaming, sizzling
Piling, patterning, under-running, water-falling
Galloping, subsiding, rolling, mottling as marble
and veining, climbing as a fountain, shivering
and leaping, in colour as smoke, as steel, as snow
Faster, and faster with the ship she goes.
Sailing, I watch her, oblivious to all I and She
Alone on earth in unity.

(Crossing the Atlantic on *Queen of Bermuda*, July 1962.)

The Movie . . .
1982

The Big Fisherman

The Big Fisherman, Peter—and as the crowd surged upward toward Christ on The Mount—I too—my soul surged forward to that Voice. Just as 2,000 years ago, the soul of the crowd went forth to Him. I was there
Backward in Time
I was there.

Haiku
(Western Style)

Twilight

Dog bark. Bell chime.
Child call. Evening cool.
All melt in Twilight's pool.

When

Rose red on green bough
Spring here
Love come any moment now

Stillness

In gardens at Twilight,
there is unutterable peace
in the beauty of the stillness.

Silence

Twilight star, homing bird
Speak to my heart
without a word.

Soon

Glory green June
Soon
Honeymoon.

Also

A swallow
slow
swoops low
follow follow follow.

Look

See!
Glory Flash
Of a bluebird's wing.

Look

See!
Little ground doves
Waddling gray-ly along.

Never

The cardinal sings
Unto his mate
Never late. Never late.

Artistry

Trees—painted stillness
Etched
Against the sky.

Flirt

Wind, crude lover
Tosses blossoms
To flirt the grass.

Sickle

I *felt* Time pass
I *heard* his sickle sweep
The summer grass . . .

Etching

Stark poetry
of a winter tree
etched against the sky.

Fallen

Fallen blossom—loveliness
Does it too
Have sad-nesses?

Hurt

Love-withered rose
With
Living thorn.

Les Oiseaux de Paradis

Les Oiseaux de Paradis
Planted by my Beloved's hand for me.
To bloom eternally.

Alive?

The trees stand
With painted stillness
In the misty morning.

Gladness

The mist-lost winter stars
Gladden our hearts
With sudden shining.

Same

Sweetly-rich as temple bell
Aves in cathedral vast
Uprising.

Planet

Wingéd, ringéd Jupiter
My star to wish For You
For You.

Settle

The pigeons wheel
and slowly settle
On the rooftop.

Gift

The fallen blossom
Gifts itself
A bouquet to the grass.

Swirl

The fallen leaf
Wizens
In a swirl of beauty.

Poverty

The night bird
Sings unto his mate
While, I, without, wait.

Day Long

All day long
My rock-fern remains
Dawn-dew en-dia-mon-ded.

They

Twilight star and homing bird
Speak to my heart
Without a word.

Peace

The mystic heart of Night
In pure silence
Holds untainted Peace.

Two

Night closes
The window
Of the Day.

Quintessence

The floating dance
of the petal of Spring
Holds the quintessence
Of everything

Much

We are told that we
are made from dust
If, I, indeed
am made from dust
Then dust is much.

Quo Fata Ferunt

Vibrations on the Winds of Fate . . .
Successive pilots of the Barque of State
Change helm . . . "Quo Fata Ferunt"
And yet, 'tis time and eras new
Not citizens erode the royal state
Of Kings.

In Bermuda . . .
"It all depends on who you are!"

Symphony

From Musson's Point
The tree-frogs commence to sing
Joining orchestra at In-ver-rurie
They become a symphony.

Hope

I stuck my nose into a blossom
A bee there too
I hope he dies
Before I do.

Oleander

Frou-frou of oleander
Pink, on the wind
Would-be rose

Which?

The silence
Speaks
Strangenesses.

Glory Be

This May morning
A perfect blossom
Smiled on me.

Question

Am I no more
Than a dried blown leaf
In the wind of things?

Is It

And is it warm beneath the sod
For those on their way
To God?

Life

Matters not how evanescent
The bud of Spring maybe
Life's a full-blown rose.

See

See!
Bare poetry
of a winter tree.

There

Naked poetry
winter tree
'gainst Creator's easel sky.

Hold

I, tempest-tost
Reach for the creator's hand
And hold.

Spring

The cardinal on
The highest bough
Sings of Spring enow.

What?

Trees, gentle-patterned
'gainst the Twilight sky
What are you saying?

Reverse

Me!
alone I walk . . .
with butterflies for company.